WHILE
THE
EARTH
SLEEPS
WE
TRAVEL

WHILE
THE
EARTH
SLEEPS
WE
TRAVEL

Stories, Poetry, and Art
from Young Refugees Around the World

AHMED M. BADR

Andrews McMeel
PUBLISHING®

ADVANCE PRAISE FOR

WHILE THE EARTH SLEEPS WE TRAVEL

"*While the Earth Sleeps We Travel* is a moving compilation of stories of refugees who each have a powerful story to tell but also have much in common. What makes this book so much more powerful is that rather than describe them, Ahmed Badr gives these refugees a chance to tell their own story in their own way . . .

As the world continues to grapple with the highest number of refugees and internally displaced people on record, this book converts statistics into names and individual stories that should and do matter. It will leave you feeling sadness at the suffering millions endure, but also filled with hope in learning about these exceptional individuals."

—Mina Al-Oraibi, Iraqi journalist and editor in chief of
   The National Newspaper

"Ahmed Badr's personal experience has thrust upon him a sense of social responsibility found in persons far in advance of his age. This collection forms a mosaic of talents from various backgrounds including some groundbreaking poetry and art by teenagers and young adults whose talents have been dismissed and neglected for far too long."

—Sultan Sooud Al-Qassemi, Founder, Barjeel Art Foundation

"These are precious stories, which have been carefully collected and sensitively told. Badr exposes the richness, diversity, and sheer beauty of the inner worlds of young people who have experienced displacement."

—Hassan Damluji, Deputy Director, Bill & Melinda Gates
   Foundation, and author of *The Responsible Globalist*

"Ahmed shows that the creative spirit of a person forced to flee or compelled to migrate cannot be squelched by bombs, confinement, or fear. In giving young uprooted people this platform to express their singular experience through words and art, he also connects them and himself to all of humanity. With his own stirring poems and art woven through, it is clear his own refugee childhood gave him the impetus to become the remarkable artist he is, but also to inspire the incredible talent of the voices reflected in the work on each and every page of this treasure of a book."

—Melissa Fleming, Under-Secretary-General for Global
   Communications, United Nations

"This collection of life-affirming artistic expressions from youth around the world is a testament to the power of storytelling and the many beautiful contradictions that the liminal spaces of identity politics can often embody. In his role as both witness and facilitator, Ahmed Badr has done a brilliant job of weaving his own poignant reflections throughout this book, while uplifting the voices of his peers in a generous and thoughtful way. As an immigrant from Syria who began my own poetic journey during my teenage years, I am in awe of these young people who are facing such profound challenges with levels of eloquence, vision and resolve that usually take a lifetime to muster."

—Omar Offendum, Syrian-American poet and rapper

"This book is an extraordinary showcase of international creativity—the power of the expressions featured transcends any borders or tragedies and serves as a vital reminder that displaced young people must be allowed to claim their place on the world's biggest stages. Ahmed Badr recognizes the inextricable relationship between agency and storytelling and is on the forefront of helping others do the same. By thoughtfully and delicately highlighting the unrestrained creative potential of resilient young people, this book invites a more critical engagement with the differences we assume about one another, and the distances we can bridge by sharing our own stories."

—Benj Pasek, Tony Award-Winning composer of
Dear Evan Hansen

"One of Ahmed's poems explores why he survived the bomb that destroyed his childhood home. It says, 'tragedies always end with a period, but yours ended with a semicolon.' This book is what comes after the semicolon. The chorus of voices of young people from places as diverse as Venezuela, Somalia, Syria, and Bangladesh, will reaffirm your faith in human resilience and challenge your assumptions about what it means to be a refugee."

—Ari Shapiro, Host, NPR's *All Things Considered*

FOREWORD

BY BEN STILLER

If I'm being honest, Ahmed Badr made me very uncomfortable the first time I met him. At eighteen, he was smart, outgoing, apparently extremely talented, and worst of all, charming. We were at a United Nations World Refugee Day event at the UN headquarters in New York. It was a big deal. He was so relaxed and composed. What was with this guy? I mean the *Secretary-General* was standing right next to us. I was sweating. Extremely nervous. Why was I even there? I had a reason. I was asked to speak about refugees and to introduce Ahmed. I was a newly appointed Goodwill Ambassador for the UN Refugee Agency, tasked with drawing attention to the dire situation of displaced people all over the world who are forced from their homes and families due to war and conflict. It's a serious subject, and in my new duties, I was attempting to seem as sober and serious-minded as possible (for a person not really known for that).

I was introduced and nervously stepped up to the podium and fumbled through some facts and thoughts that came out reasonably intelligent sounding, if not quite as clever as they seemed on the cab ride there. Thankfully done, my heart rate finally started to descend, and I watched Ahmed step up and effortlessly and simply begin to read his piece. And it immediately made me laugh. Which was not what I was anticipating. I was caught so off guard I tried to stifle it, but then saw others reacting similarly. Even the Sec-Gen was smiling. In his brilliant and unexpected poem, "A Thank-You Letter from the Bomb That Visited My Home" Ahmed conveyed humor, irony, and empathy.

Speaking from the bomb's point of view that had ripped into his childhood home in Iraq, he disarmed the audience and gave us a deeply personal experience of his world. By the end, the entire crowd was silently at attention and genuinely moved. He told his story in a way that only a person who experienced it could.

And that is the aim of this book. For too long refugees have not been empowered to share their stories. Yes, there are people like me, who try to use whatever platform we might have to shed light on the issue. We travel and meet with displaced families all over the world, and then go off and talk about it to whoever is willing to listen. We testify to governments and speak on podcasts. Any way we can get the message out to people who might make a difference. And it works to an extent. The fact is when you present the personal story of a person, a human being going through an ordeal, and not just a statistic or a number, it can move people to want to help. But no matter what I or any "advocate" for refugees might say, we will never know what it feels like.

It's a tenuous time on our planet. Major conflicts have gone on for years in the Middle East. In Central and South America, poverty stokes gang violence in countries where civil authority is weak, and in many countries, extremely corrupt. And the people who are the collateral damage—the ones directly affected—are marginalized. Worse yet, they are turned into fodder for political leaders to stoke the fear we as humans can be prone to, the fear of people who don't look or sound like us. If you have not experienced being the object of that fear, how can you understand it? How can you empathize and help others connect to our true commonality as humans on this planet?

One way is through art and the personal expression of refugee artists who can move us in a way that no one else can. That is who this book celebrates. I'm happy to say I got over my issues of insecurity with Ahmed and all that comes with his genuine sweetness and natural coolness, and we have settled into a nice friendship. I've watched in honest amazement at his total commitment to his mission. In the short time he has been a legal adult, he has done so much to highlight the voices of refugees. This book is a part of that work. He introduces us to vibrant young people who are creative and inspired, wildly talented, and who happen to be displaced. Their stories and expressions and poems and drawings are all striking in their own way. Whether it is the work or the artist behind it, these voices are authentic and inspiring. They are ready to be heard. All we have to do is listen.

INTRODUCTION

*"We wanderers, ever seeking the lonelier way, begin no day
where we have ended another day; and no sunrise finds
us where sunset left us.
Even while the earth sleeps we travel.
We are the seeds of the tenacious plant, and it is in our
ripeness and our fullness of heart that we are given to the wind
and are scattered."*

—Kahlil Gibran, *The Prophet*

Baba told me that stories are like windshield wipers during a storm; they won't get rid of all of the rain, but they will make our way clearer.

Two weeks before my eighth birthday, he told me that our house was bombed. A week later, our family left Baghdad, and we found our way to Aleppo. Back then, before the Syrian civil war, Aleppo was a beautiful city, teeming with life and safety.

The word refugee is usually associated with both an ending and a beginning. An ending in that it represents the loss of a previous life, a previous security. The ending forces us into a kind of new beginning, one in which we must completely recreate our present in hopes of a better life.

What happens in between is often ignored, and that is why the refugee narrative needs to be redefined and given a three-dimensional, realistic human face. At the time, I did not understand why our house had been bombed. I did not understand why wars were necessary and why we couldn't go back home. The word "refugee" was foreign to me.

After two years in Syria, my family was faced with a tough choice: stay there and struggle financially, or go back home and sacrifice our safety. My parents could not find jobs in Syria, and Iraq was unsafe. Mama and Baba both worked as civil engineers in Baghdad for twenty-four years and were on paid leave, which was about to expire.

Sometimes we briefly returned to Baghdad to visit family. On one of those long bus rides, my father spoke to the driver about our situation and learned of a United Nations refugee program that would take approximately 1 percent of everyone who applied and relocate them to the United States or United Kingdom. We didn't have anything to lose, and so we applied. A little over six months later, we received a phone call.

I heard my mother screaming from the living room. I ran to her, worried that something horrible had happened. She picked me up in her arms, gleefully announcing that we had four one-way tickets to Sioux Falls, South Dakota. I was ecstatic, and I assumed that Sioux Falls was just a cab ride away.

We tried to figure out how to pronounce the name of our new home and eventually came to realize that the "x" in "Sioux" was silent. We landed in America on May 19, 2008.

Over the past few years, I've begun to retell my family's story. The current political climate and the anti-Muslim, anti-refugee sentiment that comes along with it have forced me to examine our past through a new lens.

After a year in America, my parents went back to college to reevaluate their master's degrees. In 2012, we moved to Houston, Texas, my parents hoping they could find jobs in their field. At this point, they had been unemployed for three years, so they found minimum-wage jobs to keep the family financially afloat. During these years, my mother fought and won a battle against breast cancer, and we have all become American citizens.

Those were some of the best times of my life. I learned about the true value of perseverance and realized that the fight for survival had many faces.

What if, when you heard the word "refugee," you thought of a neighbor, a coworker, or someone who was simply trying to figure out how to pronounce "Sioux"?

For far too long, the global conversation around the refugee crisis has excluded the voices of the refugees themselves. During my freshman year of high school, a friend suggested that I write about my family's journey. At the time, I didn't really understand what a story was or that we had one worth telling. All I knew was that it was pretty confusing to be an Iraqi-American-Muslim-refugee, and I wanted an outlet that would help me understand my identities, the ways they intersected and clashed.

I began with the stories that were beginning to slip away, the moments reminding me of childhood's greatest joys. The form did not matter; the memories had to be collected, made immortal so they could be called upon later.

A year after this process began, I received a scholarship to attend the Washington Journalism and Media Conference held at George Mason University. The conference presented a week of workshops, tours, and speeches by leading American journalists from the country's top news outlets.

The conference organizers suggested that each attendee (or National Correspondent, as they called us) create an online blog they could populate during and after the program. I went all out, buying business cards and reserving a .com domain. I called it Mesopotami, and I started uploading poetry, photography, and short essays. In the Arabic language, a letter akin to "I" is used to signify ownership. I wanted to hold on to Iraq and its beauty, so I took its ancient name, Mesopotamia, and made it my own.

That week in Washington, DC, changed everything. For the very first time, I was able to see how empowering storytelling could be. All of a sudden, I realized that my exploration of the Iraqi-American-Muslim-refugee experience could be helpful to those who were going through similar crises. More important, we acquired strength when all of those identities intersected. I was among people of many identities that rarely blended—it was my responsibility to make each connect with the others.

A year after the conference, I decided to create Narratio, an online platform that publishes the poetry, art, and stories of young people across the world, with a focus on highlighting the voices of refugees and immigrants. After Mesopotami was born, a whole new world of expression opened. With Narratio, I wanted to make this world accessible to as many young people as possible.

In the past five years, Narratio has published the work of nearly 200 young storytellers from over 15 countries, conducted storytelling workshops across the United States, Greece, Italy, and Trinidad and Tobago, and launched a Fellowship program for resettled refugee youth in partnership with the Metropolitan Museum of Art and Syracuse University.

This book is structured like the Narratio platform, including poetry, art, photography, and narrative. These works were collected through workshops and interviews in camps, community centers, sidewalks, coffee shops, and parks in Greece, Trinidad and Tobago, and Syracuse, New York. The story of our work is only just beginning, and this book is both a catalogue and an invitation. It is a catalogue of the creative expression we have unleashed and an invitation to you, the reader, to join us in empowering the world's young people, displaced or otherwise.

Throughout the process of putting the book together, I struggled to choose which of my personal poems to include or whether to include any at all. My own role has shifted so many times—writer, interviewer, workshop leader. In the end, I chose the poems that best aided my understanding of my own personal story and how it related to the quickly changing world around me. These specific poems, distinguished by a yellow background, were written over a span of six years, and each captures sentiments that inspired my earliest thoughts about the book. I include them not to centralize my role in it, but to serve as a guide and a mediating force for the other works included. I have been very privileged to be able to share my story with millions around the world, and this book is ultimately an attempt to inspire more communication like it.

The following pages mark an introduction to a powerful range of voices: refugee youth from Iraq, Syria, Afghanistan, Somalia, Palestine, Kenya, Venezuela, Sudan, Bangladesh, and Iran—all taking back the microphone and the airwaves, the pen and the paper, the brush and the canvas—shaping their own representation and proving that their voices stretch beyond the walls of a camp or the margins of their asylum documents.

Together, we are speaking up and proclaiming to the world that our existence is worthy of its attention. We are the narratives of the narratives, the stories of the stories, and the humans not behind the numbers, but in front of them.

So here's a glimpse of the forgotten middle, refugee youth who are preparing to take back their narratives, using storytelling on their own terms.

CONTENTS

For Maytham, Hanaa, and Maryam, and the millions of parents and children whose stories transcend their displacement.

AHMED M. BADR

FREQUENTLY ASKED QUESTIONS
TO AN IRAQI REFUGEE

Is Osama bin Laden your cousin?

No. But I have a cousin named Osama. You should get to know
him—he loves Americans and their questions.

You're from Iran, right? Or is it Iraq? I always get them mixed up.

Let me make it easier for you:

Think weapons of mass destruction. Think George Bush.
Think lies.
Think war on terror.
Sorry.
War of terror.

**How did you survive the war? It must've been so hard for you and
your family, living under such a brutal dictator.**

Sometimes, I forget who was brutal. I forget whose side brutal was
on. Brutal kept showing his face on the news, so I assumed he had
friends on both sides.

I

You must have so many stories! Did you talk about any of them in your college essay? Oh my God, you would get in everywhere!

Actually, you know the Common Application, where you go to apply for college? You can attach files to your submission. I tried to upload some weapons of mass destruction, but for some reason I just couldn't find any.

Do you consider yourself Iraqi-American?

It's a label I struggle with. Some days I wake up not knowing whether I'm the conquered or the conqueror. In 2003, a rifle was pointed at me. In 2008, we moved to America, and suddenly I was the one holding it.

This time I was pointing the rifle at my old identity, asking it why it always mispronounced English, why it thought there was a difference between freedom and democracy, asking it whether it thought Arabic was written from right to left to confuse the West, and asking it if the Mississippi ever heard of the Euphrates.

In an interview with CBS News on September 12, 1996, Secretary of State Madeleine Albright was asked the following question:
"We have heard that half a million children have died [in Iraq]. . . . Is the price worth it?"
She replied, "We think the price is worth it."

I recently found out that Secretary Albright teaches at Georgetown. I was rejected from Georgetown. My application essay was 500 words long, but I wanted to write 500,000.

Growing up, Mama always told me, *el maerof yergos iegol al gaa oja*. "Those who can't dance always say the ground is crooked."

Mama, it's hard to dance because the ground has 500,000 cracks whispering under my feet.

They're telling me their names, ages, stories, and asking just how many cracks a medal is worth.

An Invitation to the Displaced

We are representations of a past we were deprived of embracing,
planets framing a lonely moon painted by the chosen few.
Rough and soft hands,
empty,
clasped fists shaping stories until the spaces between
our fingernails begin to whisper:

You were meant to be here earlier, but welcome to your
rightful place. Write as you wish, tell your stories, I will
gather your audience.

Nurallah Alawsaj, 20
Iraq, Palestine

Nurallah considers herself to be a photographer first and a poet second. She views both media as opportunities to tell her own story and the stories of those in her community. As a college student approaching her senior year, she hopes to continue writing more poetry, shooting photographs, and pursuing a career in acting and performance.

نحن راجعون
("We Are Returning")

Can I free you?

I have been imprisoned for years hoping to escape one day.

You didn't choose to have me here . . . yet you never took a step toward me.

You complained that you tried to connect with me.

But have you really?

I have been touched by many hands but not once by yours.

Why can't you just stop and realize you have lost me?

I am your soul trying to connect with you.

Can you free me?

You're the person I want to be. You're the one who knows me.

I can't wait any longer to meet.

Can I free you?

Can you free me?

What's the difference?

Erwin Zareie, 28
Iran

"Everywhere you go, the sky is the same."

Erwin is one of the most selfless humans I have ever met. We spent
several hours together traveling around Athens, going from his
favorite coffee shop to an artist collective that houses his studio to
a park bench, where we had the following conversation.

His voice is quiet and measured, and his eyes twinkle behind a
set of round glasses. Erwin is dedicated to raising awareness about
homelessness throughout Athens, and he is committed to creating
resources to share with the city's most vulnerable communities.

*The following narrative was assembled by the author based on an
in-person interview with Erwin. The interview was conducted in
English.*

I learned English by listening to music.

I love Queen; I love rock music. At first I listened to rap music, artists like Eminem, and then I moved on to pop, mainly Michael Jackson. When I found rock, I found heaven.

Queen is my favorite. As a kid, I would find each song's translation, put on my headphones and hold the lyrics in my hands, and sing along to "Bohemian Rhapsody," "Love of My Life," "The Show Must Go On," and "We Will Rock You."

I left Iran because of political problems. During college, I noticed how gender inequality manifested itself in our society. I got together with a group of friends, and we wrote about this inequality, sharing our work on the street.

Five months later, I was arrested. My passport was blocked for travel, and I was in prison for three months. I decided to find a smuggler and escape to Turkey. After several unsuccessful attempts, I made it across the border.

I stayed in Turkey for six months. Regarding government assistance, all I got was a piece of paper from the asylum service, and then I was on my own.

I found work at a bakery, but I didn't have citizenship or the right work papers so I could only work the night shift from midnight to eight in the morning. People knew I was a refugee because I couldn't speak Turkish, and my exhausting efforts to find a job also made me more likely to be considered a refugee. It was very hard work for little money, but I was able to survive and sustain myself.

I worked for six months and saved about 2,000 euros so I could go to Germany. I had decided to pay a smuggler to lead me to a better life. He told me that he was going to send me to Greece first, and from there, someone would meet me and take me the rest of the way to Germany.

I traveled by sea to the Greek island of Chios. There was no one waiting to take me to Germany. I had no money—the 2,000 euros all went to the smuggler. Just like in Turkey, I had to start over and find a job. At that time, all you needed to leave the island was a plane ticket to Athens, about seventeen euros. I didn't even have that much. I stayed in a camp right by the sea and saw ships come and go as I tried to find work.

So I went from coffee shop to coffee shop offering to work for two or three days and earn enough money to leave the island. After being rejected several times, I was able to scrape together twenty-five euros and buy a ticket to Athens.

I've been here for the past two and a half years. During the first few months, I wanted to pursue the same goal I had in Turkey—save enough money and travel to Germany. But when I first arrived, I was one of the homeless people. I had no money. I had nowhere to go. My English was really poor, and I slept in Victoria Park for almost a month. At that point, there weren't many camps or squats.

Every night I slept in the park. I thought about my future, and how badly I wanted to change my present. I did not want to be homeless for the rest of my life; I didn't want to sleep on the street. One night, I decided I had to help myself and other people as well. I thought about what I had, instead of what I didn't have.

I had a phone. I started studying the living situation for other refugees and the homeless population in Athens. I told myself, "God sent me here." Since my college days in Iran, I wanted to be somewhere I could help people however I could. So why not stay here and do that? Why should I go to Germany and have a normal life while people are suffering all around me? I started photographing what was going on around me and sharing my work on Facebook. People commented on my photos, and one couple asked, "What do you need? We will be in Athens next month." I replied, "A camera."

As promised, when they arrived they gave me my own camera. I continued taking pictures of the refugee and homeless situation in Athens, and many people wanted to support my work. I was approached by a woman who wanted to exhibit my photos. I remember thinking to myself, "These are all photos from my phone—they are not worthy of an exhibit!" I hadn't even learned to use my new camera.

I decided to take a chance and agreed to the exhibit. So many people came! They were very interested in the photos, and I started a dialogue about the communities I was photographing.

One night, I saw a photography contest on Facebook, and I quickly applied. I submitted two pictures with captions. A few weeks later, the organizers contacted me on Facebook to say I had won the competition. They invited me to travel to the European Commission to accept my prize. And then they asked me for my passport.

I asked them if it was okay that I was a refugee, and told them I'd never traveled with a passport before. They were a bit scared and asked me, "Are you sure you can't travel?" I answered, "Maybe you could ask!" They eventually replied and reassured me that I would be allowed to travel. When I went to the airport in Athens, I was 100 percent sure they would prevent me from flying, but they didn't! Being on that plane was like a dream. I wanted to cry. When your home tells you to go away and another place lets you be free, it is amazing. After three years of being a refugee, I was able to get a passport and travel freely. I accepted my prize, which included an all-expense paid Interrail Pass to travel around Europe.

I will begin my journey soon, and I look forward to taking more photos.

Erwin's winning submission

For the past two years, I have been collecting clothes, shoes, food—whatever they have—from churches and other organizations and distributing it to those in need.

Now I want to do something more effective. I am going to save money and buy the necessary supplies myself. In the future, I hope to rent a place where homeless people can gather and have a safe place to stay. It will be a place where they can shower, take cover, have some activities, and develop their language skills. These are necessities as much as food and toiletries.

I always have spare change in my pocket, so instead of using it to buy coffee or water, I save the change, whether it's ten or fifty cents, to buy supplies. I posted on Facebook and encouraged my friends to do the same. Even one euro can go a long way, especially in Athens where food is cheap. That one euro could prevent someone from sleeping hungry.

My fundraising started with five or six people, but now I have people who send me 500 or 600 euros. They don't even ask me to send the receipt for my purchases anymore. They trust me and know that the money goes directly to people who need it, refugees or homeless.

Many volunteers come here for one or two weeks at a time. They mean well and want to help, but they really don't know how to do that. A lot of money is wasted because no one asks the people what they need. Some volunteers rent apartments for refugees, and I always tell them, "Please don't do that." A few days ago, three families left a nearby camp because they heard that a volunteer was going to rent a home for them. It did not happen, and now they're sleeping on the street.

This is not the way to give aid. Why not help the family members by getting them English lessons or by giving them a new fan, a new bed, something that they can use in the future?

There was another situation where some volunteers decided to buy a trampoline for some refugee kids. I told the volunteers the camp really needed food and supplies, but they didn't listen to me. They wanted to prove to friends back home that they were making a difference, and they took a photo of the kids on the trampoline. An image of the kids with full stomachs wouldn't have been as powerful, apparently.

The trampoline broke after one week, and just like that, 200 euros were wasted. That money could have gone to buy so much food and supplies. Instead of giving people something temporary, we have to provide them with skills or objects that can help make their lives easier in the long term.

I believe everyone has a skill or talent. I am really bad at math, but I love learning languages, I love art and creative expression. We have to find out what people like and need and use that to help them toward a better future.

There are a few other people who have made the same decision that I have to stay in Greece and help out. But there are not very many. This is understandable because people have to provide for their own families and make sure their children have a good future. Even for Greek people, it's tough to provide for their families because of the country's poor economic situation.

For me, a simple life is good enough. I help people as much as I can through translating, teaching, or distributing materials, and that is enough. If I have a little money to pay for rent every month, that is okay. We don't know what will happen tomorrow, so why save so much money today?

Everywhere you go, the sky is the same. Please don't dream about the next place where you want to be. Life is not always better on the other side. A friend of mine told me to pray that his family could travel to Germany. Once they arrived there, they asked me to pray that they could go to Canada. No matter what country you are in, you can always find a way to make a difference.

Last year, an American college here in Athens began advertising a scholarship on Facebook. The program would accept eighty to ninety refugees for two or three semesters. I applied and was eventually accepted. I hope they will continue the scholarship, and I can finish my studies for the next four years. For the next stage of the program, only twenty students will be chosen. I hope I am one of them.

During one of my classes, I gave a presentation about happiness. As I did my research, I found that the most important things in life are being with family, having meaningful relationships, and being around people you love. I hadn't realized that before. I thought that happiness had to do with money, having a job, and a good place to sleep. Now I know how blessed I am to have people who care about me.

I may only have money for one, two, or three days, but my friendships will last for a lifetime. My brother got married a few months ago, and I couldn't be there. My parents are still working; my mother is a nurse, and my father is a chef. I dream of seeing them again someday. Not in Iran because I cannot go back there, but maybe in another country. Even if only for a few days.

"One Act of Random Kindness at a Time": Photographs by Erwin Zareie

Lina Habazi, 21
United States, Palestine

Lina believes in the power of duality—the ability to be multiple things at once while bringing together communities that might otherwise be divided. As a Palestinian-American, her work seamlessly combines her intersecting identities and opens new avenues for the preservation of memories, histories, and stories.

The following features Lina's artwork and her corresponding reflections.

Artwork by Lina Habazi

A Woman's Voice Is a Revolution

In this poster, I wanted to address expectations and misconceptions about Arab-American women. Oriental stereotyping influences society's ideas about women from the AMEMSA (Arab, Middle Eastern, Muslim, and South Asian) regions and the phrase "صوت المرأة ثورة" ("a woman's voice is a revolution") is the perfect rejection of those ideas. A woman's voice has the power to transform narratives.

Being born and raised in the United States, I have learned to proudly express my identity in a way that fuses both my American and Palestinian sides. It is often expected that women who are caught between two identities would be better off choosing one and completely losing touch with the other, but that is not necessarily the right way.

In this piece, I challenge what the woman with dual identities should look like by portraying the combination of my American and Palestinian cultures through fashion and self-expression. This poster was created with the goal of resisting orientalism. To me, that means reclaiming my identity from those who choose to define it for me. As an Arab-American, Muslim, hijabi woman, I am no stranger to stereotypes. Growing up, I have always needed to explain my identity and the reasons why I dress, speak, and believe the way I do because society generally has a distorted idea of who I am. By reclaiming my identity, I define it in a way that offers a true representation of myself.

Intersections I

Intersections II

These two pieces came out of my experimentation with new ways of portrait drawing. The overlapping elements, including pieces of others telling their own stories, allow me to uncover the underlying story that connects us all.

Grandfather

This drawing was inspired by my memories of family get-togethers in Jordan and Palestine when I was a child. My cousins, siblings, and I spent the night hours learning and playing new card games. Our cousins taught us Arab card games, and we taught them American card games. I created my version of a playing card using characters and imagery from my memories. This card features the grandfather figure as the king card with the word "grandfather" written in Arabic. I used the pomegranate to substitute for the heart suit because it was a prominent object in my childhood. I plan to continue this series with a queen (grandmother), jack (boy), and maybe an ace card with other fruits or plants as the suits.

Portrait of a Storyteller

In this piece, I wanted to illustrate the senses that are used in storytelling. Recently I've been thinking more and more about our family stories and how important it is to learn about and document them. As soon as our elders leave us, their stories and knowledge leave with them. I visualize this as a cycle: we see people, places, and events through our eyes; we listen to peoples' stories through our ears; we tell our own stories and retell those we've heard through our mouths. Each panel in this print is a different size, and they shrink toward the bottom, ending with a sealed mouth. It is meant to convey the idea that when we stop seeking out and telling stories, the life cycle of the storyteller is ended, and we lose the stories that span generations.

Maklouba

My favorite Arab dish is *maklouba*, so naturally I had to paint it.
Food was one of the first exposures I had to Palestinian culture
when I was very young. I was a picky eater so not everything
impressed me, but *maklouba* was one of the exceptions.

Solve Manson, 23
Iran

Solve always seems to smile before he speaks. Throughout our conversations, he described his life in a matter-of-fact way, occasionally pausing to tell a joke or two. A bodybuilder, chef, and photographer, he has used each of his passions to better understand and capture the world around him.

He recalls unimaginable pain and horror with potent optimism and continues to dream, hope, and imagine a future that he himself shapes and controls.

The following narrative was assembled by the author based on an in-person interview with Solve. The interview was conducted in English.

It was my Instagram page that got me in trouble in Iran. I was seventeen or eighteen when I started it. I loved photography, and I practiced it at home and in the streets in Iran. I took my first photo seven years ago. My Instagram page is political, but it also includes religion. At that time, I was reading a lot about religion, and I didn't like it. And after I made the page, I met other people who felt the same way that I did.

After two years, the page became a problem. One day, my father called me when I was at work and said, "Don't come home, just go." I wanted to delete the Instagram account but couldn't because I had forgotten the password. I went to stay with a friend who lived in the country. Within a week, I made my way to Iran's border with Turkey. It took me three hours to get across. Then I went to Bulgaria, where I spent six months in jail.

I was supposed to enter Bulgaria with a small group. We were to meet someone at the border who would bring us into the country. I was told there would be six of us, and it would take about six hours of walking. When I got to the border, there were twenty people with me, not six. I thought it wasn't a problem, and I just kept walking and walking. I was over 160 pounds then. I was big—not fat, but big. I didn't rest at all. I got into a fight with the smuggler, but he didn't listen to me. We stopped for a bit, and I fell asleep.

I woke up in the hot sun, and there was no one around me. They had left me. I ended up spending six days in the jungle without any food. I was only nineteen. I found a sign that said Bulgaria is here and Turkey is there, so I headed toward Bulgaria. After traveling for six days, I found a road.

I spent the night sleeping on the side of that road, and then five policemen and their six dogs woke me up. They asked, "Why are you alone? Are you with a smuggler? Are you a smuggler? Where are your refugees?" I told them I didn't have refugees, I was just lost in the jungle. They put me in a car, and we drove to the police station.

I spent the night there. I had no food and barely any water. At one point I told the guard I had to go to the toilet just so I could drink the toilet water. After that, I went to an immigration interview, and they said, "You are *qacaqci*. Like you are bringing people. A smuggler."

Really? At nineteen? It didn't matter. After the interview, they told me I was going to jail for six months. I thought, "Oh shit, I don't have a mobile or anything."

I spent six months in a prison with 1,500 people all in one building. Every week we had one hour of fresh air. We couldn't go outside. Only five people were from Iran; the rest were from all over—Algeria, Albania, and Bulgarians of course. Not just refugees. Some were cocaine smugglers.

My family thought I was dead. I called them after six months, and my father couldn't believe I was still alive. He had tried to call the smuggler, but he wouldn't answer. He was a friend of a friend, and I had paid him 6,000 euros.

I kept trying to call the smuggler, and he finally answered. He fought with me on the phone and promised that in one month I would be staying in Serbia. I said no problem.

After a month, he called and told me to go to Sofia on a particular bus. When it dropped me off, I should go to a certain hotel for one night. The bus dropped me off at the border of Serbia and Bulgaria, not the hotel. There were eighty people in this new group. The smuggler had turned off his mobile, so we couldn't contact him and didn't know where we were. For five days we walked about aimlessly until someone finally got the location. We were still in Bulgaria. We had been walking away from Serbia.

Three days later, we made it to Serbia and were taken to a house that belonged to the Mafia. They demanded 2,000 euros to let us leave. I called the smuggler again, and again he didn't answer. It had been days since I had any food or water. Early the next morning I snuck out of the house and went to the police. I told them everything. They went to the Mafia house and caught everyone.

Then I was put in a camp. I told them I was in danger because the Mafia was looking for me. There was a list of people who wanted to be sent to Hungary or Austria, and I put my name on it for either country. I stayed in the camp for another six months, then I went to the list manager and asked about my place. It turned out that someone had stolen the list that had my name. The boss of the camp was stealing money and identities from people in the camp.

I was deported to Croatia, then to Slovenia, and then back to Croatia. Next, I was deported to Serbia. After a week there, I tried to make my way to Hungary, but I was caught by the police. They broke my feet. It was not good.

After the last attempt to go to Hungary, I went to Romania and stayed in a home with two older people and their daughter. The daughter was scared and called the police on me. She was afraid I was putting her family in danger. So it was back to Serbia again.

In Serbia, I'm back in a camp, but I don't have a name. Man, I was angry . . . so fucking angry. After a week, I decided to go to Greece, and I've been here for two years, more than any of the other countries. When I arrived, they asked me where I was from. I told them I was from the United Kingdom. They said, "No problem, but if you're from the United Kingdom why are you so dirty?" [Laughs.]

In Iran, I had been a chef in a small restaurant. I worked very hard, from 5:00 a.m. to 2:00 a.m. I didn't have time to take many photos. But in Greece, I had more time to explore photography. I really like it because of the way it feels when I see my photos. At 5:00 a.m. I wake up to photograph the sunrise. Photos for me are like medicine. I don't want to sleep. Sometimes I go to the jungle to photograph. I like to take in the good energy there; it's relaxing.

I'm trying to keep going. Yeah, keep going. Just keep going. I've been a refugee for four years now.

Photographs by Solve Manson

Zera Qassari, 26
Syria

Zera has always been a fan of female hip-hop artists. She wrote poems but never thought of herself as a rapper. Recently, she realized that the two media are actually very similar, and she began joining the two art forms.

Psycho

Hey buddy take it slow
And let me tell you.
Living a wreck, in dirt
Such a piece of shit.
The garden is some stones that children adorned with shit.
That's why you treat me shit.
Here we go
I'm not a psycho
Just having 10 Lyrica so
I start screaming, yelling, crying
Herb smoking
I become spooky, edgy, jumpy, nervy.
My flashy and hairless neighbor comes out.
Yelling, kiddo why your voice is too loud.
Lyrica drags me down
I take a blade while I'm losing me
Hardly hear anyone
Someone says hey you squeeze, squeeze
Have some yogurt please
So you can sneeze
Again after 15 hours, I squeeze
My face is
Blue and yellow
Like a rainbow
Drink 3 in 1 after 3 in 1
Until a kettle says please I'm done.
Hey you leave me alone
Just H-O-L-D ON

Hold, hold, hold, hold on
You think you're better oh come on
You like Kim Jong Un.
So pay attention
I'm not a source of corruption.
Including I take some injection.
My therapist gives a solution.
Sertraline is your new medication.
Therapist you say
Tomorrow is another day.
Trying to convince me.
That I'm strong and not freaky.
And everything will be okay.
Though life fucks me up and my hands are tied.
Hey buddy wait a minute.
You say I'm addicted
These pills for those who no brainers.
Then you say I'm dirty.
You will make me the hot news at every tea party.
Oh . . . no, look at you.
You're not surprised 'cause you know
You are the same
You sell words.
You pretend you're not but you're a chicken.
But this time I should say.
Tomorrow is another day.
I'm strong not freaky
Everything will be okay
              will be will be okay
                    okay.

Merzad Shixe, 29
Syria

Merzad is a journalist and singer. He is one of the editors of the *Ritsona Kingdom Journal*, a multilingual, multimedia magazine produced by displaced young people.

He sees storytelling as a means of self-empowerment, and he always makes an effort to share his expertise with camp residents by holding workshops and mentoring his peers. Merzad also has a beautiful voice and enjoys telling stories through songs in Kurdish and Arabic.

Untitled by Merzad Shixe

How I see myself...

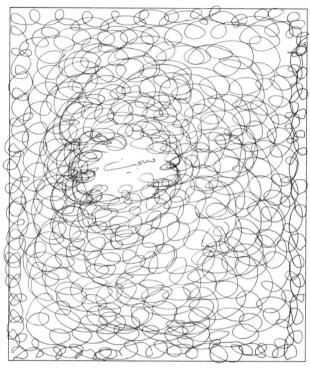

Name: Age: Country:

How I see myself:

. . . a prisoner

Translated from Arabic by the author

How the world sees me...

Name: Merzad Shikhe   Age: 29   Country: Kobani

How the world sees me:

. . . I don't care

Translated from Arabic by the author

Our Earth and Yours

Some boats ask the sea's permission before sailing.
Others have no choice but to introduce themselves
hurriedly, forcefully,
holding bodies that tell stories in dark rooms
over rusty space heaters and pristine rugs.
They say that a country lives inside a body but it will always die
outside of it.
What is a border but a stubborn scar?
A past pain that no longer persists,
but a reminder that you will never return to your previous form.
Permanence is an illusion we are forbidden to taste.

Karem Potela, 23
Venezuela

Karem is a mother and a storyteller. She is intimately aware of her personal journey and is always finding new avenues for its expression. Despite the pains of exile, she continues to maintain a strong connection with her home country of Venezuela. She hopes that through her writing she can make her daughter and the rest of her family proud.

The following narrative was originally written in Spanish and translated into English by Karem Potela.

I had to migrate as if I were being pursued by a plague, as if escaping from a telluric movement or any natural disaster— something quick and terrible from which I had to flee so I wouldn't become a victim, as so many in my country already had. I fled the terror and left everything, not just the material things but everything. I was one of the many people who could not take anything with them but some clothes and hope for a better future . . . but only when I was calm, when I finally felt that I was safe, did I realize the immensity of what I had left behind.

The most important thing I left was the affection of the people I lived with, the experiences that made me who I am today. For my people, family is important; everything revolves around it, and family provides the sense of unity that characterizes us. It is not only the close family (parents, siblings) but also the extended family and even those who are not of our blood whom we consider our own: cousins, friends, *compadres*, *panas*. Our family nucleus extends outward, and we have many family names. Skin tone and social stratum do not matter, only the deep feeling remains.

I left all of them. I can take memories with me—of the people I love, the flavor of the *chicha* that my dad or my mom bought me in the afternoons, or meetings with school classmates. But I can't take the cart where I tried that *chicha* or the schools where I studied with my classmates.

I can't take the places or the people I loved, just their memories. And some of those people, my close extended family, are also left with only memories. My older brother is in Peru. He left to seek better opportunities for helping us because in Venezuela he had no way to provide for his family. My other brothers are still in Venezuela waiting for things to change in the country or else they will have to get out. My daughter's name is Daniela; she is four years old and next month she turns five. I have not been able to bring her with me because she is not a resident and therefore is not eligible for free education. I would have to pay for a private school but the cost makes that impossible. I want her to have a future that my country will never provide, to get an education and stay away from all the bad things that happen on the streets of Venezuela. After nine months with my baby inside me, loving her, caring for her, and finally feeling how small she was in my arms, who could have known that because I love her so much I would have to leave to offer her a better future? No one.

I have left behind the places I loved and my family, the most beautiful thing in my life. Who can take away the immense emptiness inside me? My family is fine, and I always help as much as I can. But I am always worried about the people I love in a country where 91 out of 100 crimes go unsolved, where only 51 percent of families survive their poverty, and where 70 percent of children do not receive an education because they have to work to bring food home. That's not the future I want for my child or for any other child. The void in my chest has names, surnames, and faces. On bad days I weep for the distance, the emptiness, for the love of those I do not have at my side.

On very bad days I feel like I'm going crazy, that I want to leave everything here and go home to my mom, my family, my little girl. But I can't; they need me, and I have to be strong for them. I have to be strong even though I am having a hard time. How would they feel knowing how much I suffer and how bitter I feel about myself for missing them? I stand firm because all I have left is the hope that I will be with them again, holding them so tight they're grounded in my chest. I will tell them that I will never leave them again, that I love them more than anything else in this life because without them, life is not worth living. I thank my family for giving me the strength to continue every day.

Khadija Mohamed, 19
Somalia

Khadija's warmth and charisma have made her a formidable force in her community. Her journey toward self-expression has led her to curate a museum exhibit, multiple public speeches, and a performance at the United Nations.

As a Somali-American writer and community organizer, she attends Syracuse University and teaches middle school girls at a local literacy center. She focuses her writing, activism, and art on women's empowerment, cultural awareness, and promoting education for all.

Naag iska dhig
("Act Like a Woman")

As I stand here carrying food on my head,
I hope the nutrients can seep through
straight into my brain and remold what it means
to be a woman.
Naag iska dhig
As if that's to remind us that power
is placed in the hands of men.
Naag iska dhig
As if to put her in her place.
Naag iska dhig
Play the role that women have played.
But they don't know
Naag iska dhig are words of encouragement.

Hadii naag tahay sameey, they say—"If you're a woman, do it."
But as a female I rise before the sun,
saying goodbye to the night while welcoming the new day.
My hands gracefully make a feast of *anjero, beer ey shahi,*
delicately adding each ingredient without having to measure,
an art form that was passed down from *ayeeyasha*—my ancestors.

Naag iska dhig
But they don't know

I carry yesterday's workload in my joints.
I carry humanity's humility in my stomach
for nine months.
I carry the world's love in my heart,
and I carry these fruits gracefully

Where did "throw like a woman" come from?
As if we are weak,
as if every month we don't battle ourselves
and clean up the blood,

Period.

As if we can't be both gentle as ripples in a stream
and electrifying as a <u>thunderstorm.</u>

Did YOU forget
that once you were inside of me,
depending on me,
and I opened the uterus portal
wincing through the pain to get you here
So never forget!

My grandmother says, *markii lugudhalaayi dahab ayaad aheed ee ha
is raqiisinin.*
("You were born golden, don't cheapen yourself.")
Boqortooyo—royalty—runs in my blood,
and it's evident in my golden *malaab* skin.
My crown is this basket,
my jewelry is the sweat, tears,
and blood it took to get here.

Mirna Aslan, 23
Syria

Mirna believes in art's power to provide agency and self-trust. She began drawing at five years old, using colored pencils to create stories through sketches. During one of our workshops, I asked Mirna, if her art could speak to her, what would it say? She replied:

"It would say: sketch. Let out what is inside you. I am your paper, I am your colors, I am your dreams. I will make you feel in your heart and your mind that you can achieve what you want. As you get bigger, I will get bigger alongside you."

Untitled artwork by Mirna Aslan

Istarlin Dafe, 18
Somalia

Istarlin hates poetry—at least she thought she did. Before beginning to write, she viewed poetry as an exclusive thing that only older people read and wrote. She despised the fact that all of the poems she read had to follow certain guidelines and rules, all of which she had not yet learned about.

Once she realized that poems can be defined and shaped by poets rather than their audiences, she decided to give the medium a try.

The Cup of Memory

On Saturdays and Sundays she would stay with us in the camp.
I would leave with her sometimes and walk to her house.

An hour and a half by foot.

An adventure away from the camp and into the countryside.

From the hectic to the peaceful.

Away from the camp's cramped spaces, where privacy is
rare and chaos is common.

We walked on the red sand streets
where early buses drove by kicking dust.
I didn't mind the dust because we were so involved in conversation.
Occasionally we stopped to say hello to the neighbors and
people we knew.

My *ayeeyo*—my grandmother—is a gorgeous, proud Somali woman
with a clear heart.

We wake up for Fajr prayer, before the sunrise.

I can hear her whispering the *athkar*

Subhanallah
Alhamdulillahi
Astagfirullah

The *Athan,* the call to prayer, is playing in the background.

I turn to my *ayeeyo.* She's putting on her favorite black and white *baati,* a traditional dress, and her favorite black headscarf.

She grabs a jug and a cup, and we leave through the front door and make our way to the yard.

The first time I saw the camels, I thought they were grumpy.

When my grandmother touched them, they seemed to change their mood.

She turned to me and said:

"You have to learn. You have to be patient. If you don't, then the camel will start kicking, and you will get hurt."

Then she would milk the camel, and I would hold the jug. I was afraid it would start kicking. My body would shake, and I'd lose my balance.

We would fill three jugs and then sit nearby to try the milk.

She took a cup, scooped out some milk, and handed it to me.

The lines around the cup looked like the lines on my *ayeeyo's* face,

full of wisdom and patience.

It was like the cup had a unique meaning as I drank the milk.
We sat there and talked for hours.

Lessons through stories, stories through lessons.

As I sat there with my *ayeeyo*, the cup, and the warm, sweet, milk, I
told myself to always remember to be thankful and selfless.

Nakhal

Yesterday,
I saw a picture of a field of date trees
cut off at the head
where the fruit is supposed to grow.

I tasted my first date in Baghdad when I was three years old. My
father picked the fruit straight from the tree, and handed it to me. I
immediately tasted the sweetness on my fingers.

Back then, I had date-sized hands. All of the dates I tasted were
grown at my grandparents' home. We had four date trees, stretching
into the sky. One of our trees was over twenty feet tall, and we had to
hire someone to climb it when harvest season came along. The trees
had lessons within their roots.

I imagine a botanist in an elite American institution, looking at
a date tree from Baghdad. He might study and marvel at the
resilient plant, but he won't see the centuries of wisdom. He will
miss the lessons.

Yesterday, I asked my mom about dead things.

I asked why the date trees had been cut off at their heads,
and why they were drooping.

She said that they don't stand because their roots are tired.

They don't speak because their lips are in a foreign museum.

They are stuck behind a language barrier.

Mama, are date trees a metaphor for our country?

Ask your grandmother, she said. She has seen enough date trees to be more knowledgeable than all of Iraq's Parliament.

My grandmother grew up in the 1940s, when Iraq was a kingdom God still cared about.

She said, "Back then, the fruit tasted sweeter, and the date trees grew with pride.

Back then, we walked with stories on our shoulders and emptied them out at the dinner table.

Back then, you didn't just wear your clothes,
you wore your ancestors."

She told me that on Thursdays she wore Babylon and on Mondays she wore Sumeria.

She told me that on Fridays she loved wearing her favorite earrings, the Tigris and the Euphrates, the rivers that run through our country.

Today,
I saw a picture of a country
cut off from any color
going to sleep without plans for awakening.

I saw a picture of a playground
where children are supposed to play
with their date-sized hands.

Eid Ahmed, 19
Somalia

Eid is a quiet teenager with dark brown hair and a shy smile, with eagerness and curiosity that he hesitates to show. Writing was never his strong suit, yet he always knew that he wanted to preserve his family's stories. During our very first workshop, Eid led a conversation about identity in America in which he observed that his African-American classmates assumed he was born and raised in the United States. He went on to describe how his Somali background was a mark of his foreignness, but this foreignness only showed itself when he spoke.

He was having trouble deciding what to write about.

"I want to talk about my family, Somalia, but I'm not sure how to start.

My uncle used to fill cups like this with milk and then go into the city to sell them. I remember my grandmother making the cups; my siblings and I would sit around her as she took wood and carved them."

His eyes lit up, and he immediately asked, "Do memories count as poems?"

He already knew the answer.

Hooyo, ayeeyo, adeer

Mother, grandmother, uncle.

My *hooyo* told me to be home before the hyenas came.

My uncle would stay up all night as they circled the home. Hyenas were scared of humans, so he had to make sure he was seen.

Sometimes we put clothes on the trees so the hyenas would mistake them for us.

My *ayeeyo* told me we had to keep the goats safe so we would have milk to drink.

Hooyo, ayeeyo, adeer

I remember seeing my grandmother in the summer heat, sitting under the tree.

My cousins and I sat around her, watching her weave the wood into goblets. It didn't matter what size, her hands moved in rhythm so the shape would be even. Small at the bottom, and larger at the top. Small at the bottom and larger at the top.

She told us stories to keep us entertained, to keep us quiet as she worked.

Sometimes she told us to get water.

She didn't wear shoes so she would be comfortable.

She sat on the *qadiifad*, an old, worn carpet, to keep her clothes clean from the red sand on the ground.

My uncle would take the goblets, fill them with milk, and take them to the city to sell.

Both sides of the camel would be full of the goblets, each bursting with milk. Three on each side.

When he came back, he brought us candies. We always asked him when he would leave for the city again. We wanted our *nacnac*, our candies. My *adeer* always brought them for us.

Today when I talk to my grandmother, I remember her hands, the same hands that carried me and wove the goblets.

I remember all of us sleeping together in a small room.

Hooyo, ayeeyo, adeer

When the weather was cold, we would come together. My grandmother always put herself closer to the cold so we would be warmer.

Hooyo, ayeeyo, adeer

My story is my testimony. I pray that by sharing my testimony I can change people's lives and help them be courageous and strong, believing that things will work out for good.

I am living in Trinidad and Tobago, seeking asylum. I was born into a large family. My father died when I was eighteen years old. My mother is the strongest woman I've ever seen—she is my hero. She never gave up on us. She is always there, helping us as best she can, by the grace of God. Even though my mom is a very strong woman, she can not do it all alone. Raising five children at once is not easy.

I dreamed of becoming a medical doctor, but it didn't work out because our country wasn't safe, and I did not have the finances. I graduated from secondary school with nine subjects, including mathematics, English, chemistry, physics, agriculture, social studies, and Christian religious studies. As a science student, I was eligible to apply to university to study medicine, but my life changed completely in August 2014.

Our lives were very difficult, made even more so by Boko Haram. They were killing Christians, bombing churches, and kidnapping young people, especially girls. The bombings came very close to our church. Our whole family was traumatized, and we lived in fear for our lives. Even when we went to church, we were afraid because terrorist violence could happen at any time.

There were herdsmen who moved their sheep and cows from one village to another, feeding them grass. All of a sudden, they became killers who turned to attacking and murdering people. They ambushed people at their farms in the middle of the night, destroying families. Eventually, they bombed one of the largest churches in Nigeria.

I decided that I had to flee my country. I wanted to find a place that offered a better life and an opportunity for me to achieve my ambitions. Although my dreams of being a doctor have been taken away, I find joy in music. I'm a singer, songwriter, and musician. I believe I am blessed with a talent for writing songs, playing guitar and keyboard, and singing.

I decided to see if I could get a visa to the United States. It was my dream to come to America and become somebody, but it was a very difficult process. I got rejected. Someone suggested that I travel to Mexico and then smuggle myself into America. So I set up an interview at the Mexican embassy. Initially, I was rejected, but I decided to try again, and I set up a new interview.

On the morning of August 17, 2014, I left my home in Imo state to go to Abuja for the interview. Before I left, I called a friend and told him to pray for me so the interview would go well. I fell asleep to the rocking of the bus.

Suddenly, I thought I was asleep, but I couldn't really tell what was happening. I was in a different place, walking on a road. A man came up to me and said, "Bro, you've been in an accident."

How could I be in an accident? I wasn't in the bus now, so how was it possible? The man looked at me and smiled, and immediately I felt a heavy breeze, a wind, and I came back to my body. I realized I was lying on the side of the road near the bus.

I later learned that the bus driver had been speeding to pass through Enugu state at Opi, which was infamous for having a lot of outlaw herdsmen. Another bus was coming in our direction, and its driver was doing the same thing. We had a head-on crash.

Some villagers nearby heard the loud crash and rushed to the scene to rescue any survivors. My body was moved away from the bus. I had passed out, so they thought I was dead.

Before the villagers could return to the buses after removing my body, a fire exploded between them. There were about eighteen seats on each bus, and I was the only one who made it out alive.

The police arrived and took me to a nearby hospital where I regained consciousness. I had lost my memory, and the hospital staff were trying to explain what had happened. I wanted to leave the hospital right away so I wouldn't miss my interview the next day. I convinced the doctor to discharge me.

I had lost my phone, and I only had my wallet with me, so I couldn't reach out to my family. I was bleeding all over, but I decided to continue my journey. I got to Abuja around 4:00 a.m. the next day.

I was rejected a second time, and I lost hope. I thought it would have been better if I had just died in the accident instead of surviving and being denied the visa. The same friend who had told me to apply to the Mexican embassy encouraged me to apply to a country in the Caribbean. At that point, I just wanted to leave, so I submitted my passport to the Trinidadian embassy. They gave me a visa! I arrived here on October 1, 2014.

Life has been easier here, but I still live in fear of being arrested by the immigration authorities. When I arrived, I had nothing with me but my passport, a pair of shoes, pants, and a shirt, and I had trouble seeing. I started a new life even though I barely had clothes to wear. I had to survive, and I didn't have the love of my family to support me. I had nobody in Trinidad.

I got some work and was able to save money and buy clothing. Eventually, I went to school at North Eastern College to study music. I got a certificate in production and primary entry-level musical studies. With the certificate, I can produce music and sing and perform.

I also found a church I could call my own. I played keyboard for them, and soon I became the worship leader for the church, which I am to this day.

Things were going well, but I still lived in fear of being deported back to Nigeria. In January 2018, the police came knocking at my door and arrested me. They handed me over to immigration the next day. I was locked up in a cell for seven days before my whole church came crying and praying to God for my release. The congregation was able to raise 26,000 Trinidad and Tobago dollars to bail me out.

It didn't end there. I still lived in fear because I didn't know what was going to happen. The authorities had taken my passport and put me on a supervision order, which meant that I had to report to them every month. Early in 2019, immigration ordered a special inquiry about me to determine whether I could stay in the country or not. I cried to my church; I cried to God. My church prayed and fasted for me.

The special inquiry process leads to one of two outcomes: either they allow you to leave the country voluntarily, or they lock you up and deport you. There are many people who stay in the immigration detention center for years. For me, going back to Nigeria would be very dangerous, so both options made me fear for my life. Before the inquiry began, I went to the United Nations office and got my ID card as an asylum seeker. The church helped me get a lawyer, and he went with me to the special inquiry. When we arrived, the officers realized that I was seeking asylum, so they didn't have the option of giving me voluntary departure. Since I was seeking asylum, I could stay and wait for the outcome of my case. If I am taken in as a refugee, they will cancel the special inquiry. If I am not accepted as a refugee, they will send me back to my country.

So to this day, I live in fear, and I pray that Trinidad will understand my situation. The Boko Haram terrorism in Nigeria is worse, and my mother has emigrated to Gabon for her safety. My twin brother has also left Nigeria.

I am away from my home and my family, and I miss both of them deeply. But God saved me, so I believe he has a plan for me, something that will bring me a better life. I want to encourage people to realize that nothing is impossible with God and to believe that God is still working miracles.

Nidaa Aljabbarin, 19
Syria

As one half of the first set of Aljabbarin twins (the family has two), Nidaa is a natural storyteller with a love for Syrian history and heritage. Through her work, she hopes to provide a full picture of the country, one that includes not only the pain and destruction but also the resilience, beauty, and humanity within its citizens and cities.

The Day I Left

Ya beet jede, tha'a al maftah, wa bouabak tebki ala elrah.
Oh grandfather, our house key is lost, and the doors cry
for those who left.

I wake up, and my eyes immediately forget the taste of a good sleep.
I look around wondering what there is left to see.
I see my grandfather, the vessel, and the house key.

I look at the vessel, not understanding what I see.
I see my grandfather's eyes, as he prepares to face his fears.
Fears that we're all leaving, like drops of tears.

I walk out of the house not knowing why I must leave.
Everyone holds my hands, giving me something I need.
Then my grandfather asks me, "Where is the house key?"

I don't know, *jede.*
Will we be back to use this key again?
Will the doors be there to greet us?
I set foot in the street, knowing what my body needs.
My thoughts fight among themselves, bleeding into tears.

I don't recognize the look in my grandfather's eyes.
He looks as if he is about to face his worst fear.
The fear turns into a teardrop.
He takes his glasses off, but the tear is stubborn.
It refuses to leave his face.

Ya beet jede, tha'a al maftah, wa bouabak tebki ala elrah.
Oh grandfather, our house key is lost, and the doors cry for those who left.

Mayar, 12
Syria

Mayar's energy and intelligence are infectious. Throughout our workshops, she always visited the camp's playgrounds and rounded up her friends so they could also participate. For those too young to join the classes, she showed them her writing and encouraged them to take part in their own way. Mayar also mentored a few of her younger friends and held mini-workshops for them in her home.

أنا اسمي مبار   أنا من: سوريا

أنا عمري: ١٢ سنة

هويتي المفضلة : أنو اصير دكتورا اطفال

ولا هلم لي بحلم فيه ، دبس الكبر بدي أحقق هلم لي بحلم فيه انشاء الله

رح ضلي بحلمي   ورح ضلي مستمرا بهذا الشي لنو هذا حلمي لي بحلم فيه وبتمنا انو يصير هذا الشي ونشاء الله رح ادرس عن الطب لنو من اول ما كنت صغير كان عمري ٦ سنين كنت بحلم بهذا الشي ونشاء الله اذا صار هذا الشي رح ضلي مستمرا لنو هذا حلمي الوحيد حلمي ما فيني استغني عن حلمي وفيا و اذا صار هذا الشي رح كون مبسوطا وما رح

اعطي مرضتي لا هدا واهيانان انا اتخيل هالي انو صرت دكتورا طبعن انا بفكر بفكار انو كيف رح صير دكتورا اطفال.
    شكران الكون

My name is Mayar. I am from Syria and I am twelve years old.

My dream is to become a pediatrician.

That is my only wish. When I get older, I hope to achieve it, *inshallah* ("God willing"). I will keep going until I reach this goal. I am proud of my dream, and I sincerely wish that it will come true. *Inshallah*, I will study medicine because ever since I was six years old, I dreamed of doing that. *Inshallah*, if this comes true, I will keep going and not ignore my dream. If it comes true I will be happy, and I will not give my happiness to anyone. Sometimes I think about how I am going to become a children's doctor. I imagine what it will be like.

Translated from Arabic by the author

أنا هاجي انو اكون بي مكان هادي
يعني مكان ~~████████~~ بينسيني
اكون مرتاحا في لشو هوني بي لولاد
بي صلو بيصرخو ولعلم هون كلها ضايجي
وبرا في اثنا احس حالي و مرتاحا وحلمي انو
ادرس كتير كتير مشان انو اكون مبسوط بهذا
الشي طبعن بس اكبر و رح ادرس عن الطب
وكمان انا حب انو اصير دكتورا اطفال عذا حلمي
الوحيد مشان اعلج اعلج اطفال اليونان وسوريا
واصير عبقريا اخلي الدول كلها تحكي
عليا بتصير ~~████████████~~
~~█████~~ وبجاعت حلم ماما لي ضحيت
فينا انا واخواتي لي طلعت فينا من
حرب سوريا .

I would like to be in a place that is peaceful, a place where I can be comfortable. Here, the kids keep shouting and there is so much noise. Here, everyone is upset. Outside in Athens I feel more comfortable. My dream is to study medicine when I get older and become a children's doctor. It is my only dream, to treat the children of Greece and Syria. I would like to become a genius, and people from all the countries would talk about me. I would make Mama's dream come true because she sacrificed for me and my brothers and sisters when she took us out of the Syrian War.

كمين ارا نفسي هود العالم :

- مجهو بهذا الشي .
- اهب اعطي معلومات مشان تفيدهم .
- اهب مساعدت الاخارين .
- اهب احب لا اوزع بغيري
- اهب ازيد الحبا بين الناس
- اهب احترام الكبير و اعطف على الصغير
- اهب لا املك شي سياء

اهب اعطيهم ابري خاصي بهم : وجيدا لهم
اهب اعطيهم دواء يصحهم : ومفيد لهم
اهب لا اعطي هدا ادواء لاناس بو لا وهب اعطي دواء
يناسبهم مشان لا تسداد المرضا كتيرا ن وكمان نصير
العالم يحكو علينا انو هاي الدكتورا موشاطرة بس بصصها
المصاري ما بيعرف شي دكتورا ما شلة وكما بعدين
ماعد يوعلي لا بدراس طب صير اشطار دكتورا
تصير العالم تحكي علينا انو هاي دكتورا نشاطرة و بيعرفو
فيا و بيدعولي احسن ما بطلع دكتورا ناشلة

- شكرن الكون

How I see myself around the world:

I am very happy about this.

I want to give people information that will help them.

I love helping others.

I don't ever want to hurt anyone.

I want to spread love between people.

I love respecting my elders

and being kind to those younger than me.

I don't want to do anything bad.

I want to give children the special shots they need.

I want to give them the special medicines that would help them.

I don't ever want to give someone the wrong medicine,

and I would like to give everyone the correct medicine

so their illness is cured.

Maybe the world will talk about me.

They will say I am smart, and that they believe in me, and that I am not a bad doctor.

Thank you all.

A Thank-You Letter from the Bomb That Visited My Home

Dear Ahmed,

I knew that I was gonna change your life. I knew that as soon as I entered your old home in Baghdad. Your dad, Maytham, was holding your sister Maryam in the kitchen. Your mom, Hanaa, was near the dryer. I found a place between them.

You were away at your grandparents' home, so we didn't get to meet.

You didn't know this at the time, but I was a dud missile, designed to destroy but not explode.

I entered your home through the bathroom window, made my way through the walls of the kitchen cabinet, and sneaked through three natural gas canisters. You know those old-school ones your mom used for cooking? I'm sorry for leaving gaping holes through each one, I was in a rush. Good thing your dad emptied them out two days before my visit.

I've been reading your articles. I noticed that you mention me a lot, which made me very uncomfortable at first. I'm not used to being recognized.

I usually turn children like you and your sister into dust. When I meet new people, my palms tend to be bloody. Haven't you always wondered why your dad rarely spoke about me? He told you that tragedies always end with a period. Yours ended with a semicolon. You moved on to great things, but I was still there. Watching.

Most tragedies never fully disappear. They share your breath, your blood, and walk around the ridges of your ribcage when they can't fall asleep.

But you were different. For some reason I couldn't live within you. I couldn't share your breath, or your blood. You wouldn't let me.

Maybe it's because you weren't there.

I know that every night before you fall asleep, you ask yourself what would have happened if you were there to meet me.

I'm writing to thank you. Thank you for using me for good.

Know that my body changes locations without my permission. I don't enjoy meeting people. I don't relish the destruction. I am designed to collect breaths and keep them to myself. No matter which side I'm working for, this purpose never changes. Us bombs never get to choose who to visit.

You came back to visit me two years ago. You didn't see my body, of course, that was long gone. But you saw the window in the bathroom where I first introduced myself. It was now fixed, but I was still there. You were alone, and the rest of your family was outside. You took out your phone to take a picture of me, but you were out of storage. You laughed at the irony.

You put your phone down, and stared at me. And I stared back. You smiled, and then walked away.

And in that moment, I realized that your survival is my only salvation.

Mara, 8
Palestine

Mara always called me *Amoo* ("uncle"), which made me feel very old. In return, she asked that I call her Dr. Mara because she hoped to become a pediatrician someday.

When I first asked her how old she was, she held up eight fingers. I asked whether she could write that number, she laughed and looked away, embarrassed. She had not learned how to write yet.

In the illustration that follows, the top "8" is my initial sketch, and the rest are hers. We did the same with her place of birth (Palestine), and her name.

Dreams أحلام

Name: MOKPOCe8 Age: ~~~ Country: EN
PALESTINE
PALESTi

Givara, 16
Syria

Givara is fascinated with the law and its teachings. Throughout our workshops, she translated for and supported the younger girls, who did not necessarily understand poetry or storytelling and were more concerned with playing and teasing one another.

Dreams أحلام

Name: Givara

Age: 16

Country: Syria

Givara   16   syria

lawyar

Fidaa Aljabbarin, 19
Syria

Fidaa is Nidaa's twin sister, and her family is the inspiration for this poem. She writes for the family members who have passed away in an effort to immortalize their spirits by revealing the stories they never had a chance to tell. She approaches this with delicate care and responsibility, noting that every letter of every word of every line must be carefully produced and examined.

الظلام والنور
("Darkness and Light")

Keep hiding
my parents say
as we escape the light of death.

Every day
walking along roads not knowing what to expect.
Mixed feelings
mixed weather
always hoping for the best.

The light that destroyed the feeling of safety in the room
of your death.
Memories fading
pain growing
but I'm still hearing the sound of your laugh.

Seeing the light take you away, I always wondered
why?
Why do you follow us wherever we go?
Syria, Jordan, here.

I saw your shadow next to the tree.
I hoped that we could connect.
I wanted to tell you
how I hated the light for taking you away from us
but also:

I am stronger than that.
You are stronger than that.
We are stronger than that.

Do Not

Do not define us by
Our tragedy
Our pain
Our sorrow
Our people
Our flag(s)
Define us by our
Souls
Stories
The distance between our truth and yours.

Meteorite Yasan
Iran

Meteorite is an artist, rug weaver, teacher, and the oldest contributor to this book. While his youth passed by a long time ago, he remains committed to teaching younger generations and hopes to build an art center that will house workshops, programs, and galleries. For that reason, he is featured in this book. Despite the obstacles life has presented, he believes that art offers powerful forms of representation that can be wielded to make the world a better place.

The following narrative was assembled and translated into English by the author based on an in-person interview with Meteorite. The interview was conducted in Farsi and Arabic.

Each rug requires specifically colored threads. My job was to dye those threads and prepare them for the loom. I got to be very good at that.

I began painting before I worked on rugs. My art was very good, but my friends and family kept telling me it was worthless, and they didn't encourage me. They said that what I was doing held no future. But I love art so much I ignored those voices and kept working. My friends and family saw the pictures I drew, and some told me they were terrible. Others encouraged me. Because of their support, I decided to keep painting.

Whenever I finished a painting, I would just sit and look at the work. I was so proud of what I had created. I really loved it. It gave me a great feeling. I loved to feel and express myself artistically. But I could not make any money with my art. My main job was weaving rugs. Weaving is an ancient practice in Iran, almost 2,000 years old.

There are provinces in Iran and Afghanistan where women weave art into their clothes. After a period of time, I taught myself different art techniques. I did not have a teacher to help me so I developed my own expertise. I wove scenes into a canvas using the threads that I usually prepared for rugs.

Artists aren't really supported in Iran. My art depicted faces of women, so society did not approve of the work for religious reasons—it was forbidden (*haram*). My family belonged to a very religious sect (*mathhabia*), and I witnessed the many problems it caused. I decided to convert to a different religion.

Meteorite weaving a painting

I got sick and became immobile because of a problem with my leg. Also, for the past seventeen years, I have had kidney problems. For two years I did not paint or draw anything. A lot of people in my family did not love me anymore because I had converted. The illness really hurt me.

Because I was sick and had changed my religion, I could not stay in Iran anymore. So I came to Greece to seek asylum. I moved to Turkey, but I couldn't stay there either. In Turkey, I was very sick and almost died before coming to Greece.

In Greece, I saw that my art was needed and loved, and I began painting all over again. In addition to the style of painting and weaving on a canvas, I also painted on wood. We call it *Munabatkari*, but I haven't worked in that style for a long time.

I want people to help and support me so I can teach young people who want to learn these art forms. My expertise places me in a teaching role. Where I am now, there is no support for art. I want to go to Athens and find help to start a center where I can teach people.

I pay for all my supplies myself. It's very tough on my pocketbook, but I try my best. When I work, the art comes to me easily. Now I have to treat my sickness, and things are difficult.

I'm currently living in Vial camp, which is not good for a sick person, much less a sick person who practices art. I want to continue my work, and meet people who like my art and will help support me so I can be more successful. My art has changed a lot since leaving Iran. Here I can paint whatever I want. I hope my art, my practice, gets better.

My current technique of dying threads and painting with them is a bit tough because I can't find threads here. All the threads I have I brought from Iran, and I'm not really certain where they are sold here. I don't think I could afford them anyway. Even though I have such problems, I will not give up my art.

I would like to establish a learning center to teach young people who are interested in art—it could be in any city. I want to transfer my expertise to young people to make sure the practice lives on. If I don't teach it, it will disappear. It took a lot for me to learn my style—I'm sure that God helped me. I love it very much. It requires patience and resilience—trying again and again—and I want to share it with people.

Here, most refugees try to learn the language. Many say they don't want to stay in Greece and are trying to get out. They see Greece as a stepping stone, a bus stop where people get off and on. Learning art doesn't seem very important during such a temporary period. If people aren't going to stay in one place, they can't take the time to develop skills there. Also, sometimes people are intimidated by my art—it looks too difficult. It requires so much patience and resilience, but it only takes a few months to begin.

Refugees are people like everyone else. Circumstances they can't control rule over them and their countries, forcing them to seek asylum elsewhere, hoping for a better life. We can try, in our own ways, to deliver the message that refugees are decent humans.

I try not to introduce myself as a person, but I introduce my work, my art. I want to let people know that I am handicapped, but I was able to overcome the obstacles. I was able to reach the level of artist. I would like to make people happy and enjoy themselves through my art. And this is my message to others, to both the healthy and the handicapped: I may not be like you, but I have my art, and it has a message to share.

Abshir Habseme, 19
Somalia

Abshir is thoughtful, soft-spoken, and curious. At our very first
workshop, he did not utter a single word. Since writing his first
poem, he has performed publicly more than five times at local
libraries, community centers, and museums. A rising high school
senior, he is looking forward to applying to college.

Canjeero

Canjeero, much like the American pancake, was how I started my mornings.

Hooyo would go to the neighbors to borrow some *bur* if we had run out of it.

The *canjeero* was ready before we woke up.

My *hooyo* awoke before dawn and prepared the sweet dish. She would do anything to make sure we didn't go to school hungry.

As she cooked, she would recite from the Quran to fill in the silence of the morning.

Ayat al Kursi and the *hadith* of the Prophet:

بسم الله الرحمن الرحيم
اللَّهُ لَا إِلَهَ إِلَّا هُوَ الْحَيُّ الْقَيُّومُ ۚ لَا تَأْخُذُهُ سِنَةٌ وَلَا نَوْمٌ ۚ لَهُ مَا فِي
السَّمَاوَاتِ وَمَا فِي الْأَرْضِ ۗ مَن ذَا الَّذِي يَشْفَعُ عِندَهُ إِلَّا بِإِذْنِهِ ۚ يَعْلَمُ مَا
بَيْنَ أَيْدِيهِمْ وَمَا خَلْفَهُمْ ۖ وَلَا يُحِيطُونَ بِشَيْءٍ مِّنْ عِلْمِهِ إِلَّا بِمَا شَاءَ ۚ وَسِعَ
كُرْسِيُّهُ السَّمَاوَاتِ وَالْأَرْضَ ۖ وَلَا يَئُودُهُ حِفْظُهُمَا ۚ وَهُوَ الْعَلِيُّ الْعَظِيمُ.

We would still be asleep, covered not only by blankets but by the blessings of Allah.

Sometimes I would wake up early just to sit next to her, to hear her recitations and watch as she prepared the flour before it became *canjeero*.

As a child I wanted to be just like her, and so I eventually learned how to make my own *canjeero*.

She taught me how to cook with care and love.

I will never forget the first time I did it on my own.

How hard it was (or how hard it seemed to be) to get the charcoal and place it under the black plate. Layering *qoryo* under it to make sure that the fire was strong.

I was glad it hadn't rained the day before, or I wouldn't have been able to find wood.

No wood, no *canjeero*.

She sat there watching, beaming with pride, as I made *canjeero* for the family.

I still remember how my siblings smiled when I served them for the first time.

We sat there, smiling, sharing memories.

Maryam, 14
Mosul, Iraq

Maryam dreams of becoming an international soccer player someday. In the meantime, she enjoys drawing and acting. At the camp's annual play, she played a leading role in *Robin Hood*.

Untitled artwork by Maryam

How I see myself...

Name: MARYAM   **Age:** 14   **Country:** iRAP

I would like to be a soccer player, and I want to open a hospital in Iraq and make people happy. I also want to go to Germany.

(The illustration in the second half of the page depicts a side-by-side comparison between life in Iraq and Greece ["Yonan"])

Translated from Arabic by the author

Jafal Osman, 30
Sudan

When Jafal responds to a question, he always takes time to consider the larger context of his answer. Growing up in Sudan, he embraced drawing at a very young age but stopped to pursue an economics degree.

At a camp north of Athens, he rediscovered drawing and took classes to improve his skills. Jafal hopes his drawings evoke genuine emotion, representing him and his perspectives in the most honest way.

The following narrative was assembled by the author based on an in-person interview with Jafal. The interview was conducted in Arabic.

When I look at a painting, I don't just think, "This is beautiful." Instead, I think, "Why did the artist create this? What is the greater meaning?" In their work, artists present their thoughts to society indirectly, without having to speak.

I worked in electricity, construction—a lot of things. I have a bachelor's degree in economics. Emigration divided my two selves. I got into trouble with the government and was forced to leave Sudan—I wasn't safe there anymore. I went to Turkey and met a smuggler who told me life there was tough and that it was better to go to Europe; I could have a better life. In Europe, there are better human rights protections. So I tried to enter Greece, but there are a lot of risks out on the sea, and things were very dangerous. I tried five times.

I started to draw when I was a kid but stopped when I became a teenager. I didn't really have time to draw. But when I eventually got to Greece, I saw some people drawing, and they encouraged me. Here in camp there is an organization that has created a great environment for art. We have a calm room with music. I felt as if I could talk to people and express myself through my paintings. I began to love art again. People don't have to speak your language; instead, you can communicate through art. I see people looking at my art in the mini-exhibits in camp, and they are happy. My work makes them happy.

When I got to Greece, life was even harder here than in Turkey or Sudan. We lived in fear because there was a lot of tension among the people. I believe that individuals who are forced to leave their country will never have peace of mind. There is no kinder country than one's own, even when one has problems. There might be racism, people might not like you, but you have to persevere. You don't have a choice.

We all have hopes and dreams. My dream is to be able to study again, especially the English language. Then, after English, I would like to study economics, as I did in Sudan. I wish I could have stayed and worked in Sudan, but unfortunately, I had to leave. At the end of the day, I just want a better life for myself.

I've always loved learning, and here in Greece I really enjoy the discipline that comes with being a student. I've been in this camp now for eight or nine months, and every day I attend classes offered by a humanitarian organization, I Am You. I haven't missed a single one unless I'm sick or in Athens for my asylum case. I love the classes because the teachers respect and appreciate us.

I learned English in Sudan, but it wasn't a very comprehensive course. Here we practice more, even the difficult words. The teachers help, and they really make you love the language and the topic. Back in Sudan, the teachers were very strict, and we learned because we were afraid of getting a bad grade. In college, we had a little more freedom, but if the Sudanese education system helped students fall in love with the material, they would go much further and enjoy the journey much more.

I would love to study art if I am given the opportunity. I have applied for many jobs, but the national economy in Greece is not doing very well. That means there aren't many initiatives that encourage people to go into the arts.

These drawings are done based on my interests and my mood, not just my experience as a refugee—often they are inspired by films, photos, and other works I've seen. Sometimes I'm in a beautiful mood, and I end up making beautiful drawings. Other times I'm tired and feeling sad, and then I draw things that aren't as beautiful. The point is not to always make something beautiful, but to create art that shows how you feel.

Untitled artwork by Jafal Osman

Abdirizak Noor, 20
Somalia

Abdi is always joking around. Humor is his way of connecting with people from all backgrounds, and it represents his first encounter with storytelling. When Abdi began writing poetry, he found that he could embrace the medium in multiple ways and that ultimately, he could use it to effectively express the stories passed on to him by friends and family members.

Guriga

Guriga means "home" in Somali.

In my *guriga*, swords are symbols of protection
and respect.

A sword lived at my father's—my *aabe's*—side, just as
we did.

He carried it wherever he went, recognizing the power it held for him
and for our family—our *qoyska*.

He let me carry it sometimes when I was with him.

I felt its power, his power, in my body.

When I was twelve years old, a group of *tuugo*—thieves—attacked
us. They hadn't seen the *seef*—the sword—at my father's side.

But when they did, they retreated.

Father told me we had to be careful with our *Awooda*—our power.

And to remember that life and death are always just around the
corner. We never know what God wills for us, but the sword can
make a difference.

We must protect the *nolsha*—life—at all costs. The life that is yours
and the lives of others.

I didn't feel power without the sword, but when I had it, I felt like I was Superman.

Father said:

"*Xakamayanta*: control.

You *xakamayanta* the sword, it does not control you.

You control what you give to the world, but you can't control what the world gives to you.

Know what you can give, and hope for the best.

The sword is only powerful when a person is holding it the right way.

You have to hold it with responsibility and respect. You don't use it to cause fear, but to keep society safe."

Bavî Dilo, 18
Syria

Bavî was very skeptical about our first workshop and was not a big fan of the exercises. Although he tried poetry, he asked me to take a picture of this drawing he had made, featuring a quote that he deeply values.

"It is not difficult to sacrifice in order to find a friend; it is difficult to find a friend worth sacrificing for."

Translated from Arabic by the author

Jameel Khan, 18
Afghanistan

Jameel is an artist in every sense of the word. He is in a constant state of self-improvement, taking art classes on top of a very demanding academic schedule. He challenges himself by seeking inspiration wherever he goes, and he wishes to produce art that is meaningful—first to himself and then to the wider public.

Jameel has stayed in Greece, but his work has traveled around the world and now resides in private collections, galleries, and cultural institutions. He hopes that one day he can pursue art full-time and continue to learn and find inspiration at every corner.

The following narrative was assembled by the author based on an in-person interview with Jameel. The interview was conducted in English.

I don't want to sit still. I don't like to sit still.

I start with a blank paper. First I draw the structure of a face, and then I move onto the eyes and nose. The longest time it took me to make a portrait was nine hours; portraits usually take four or five hours to complete.

I have been studying high school classes for a year now, taking about fourteen subjects: English, Greek, ancient Greek, physics, biology, math—very general things. I'm also going to art school. I want to continue in both directions. I recently found a new art school where I can learn acrylic and oil painting, and I will be starting there in a few days.

My father was a businessman. He left Afghanistan for thirty years, spending time in India and many other countries. He got married and moved to Pakistan. We spent fourteen years in Pakistan, and then moved to Afghanistan for two and a half years.

Life in Afghanistan was completely different. The people and the society were different from what I had known, and the language was difficult. We were starting to get used to it after six or eight months.

Then war came. Everyone in our family wanted to leave Afghanistan, and we thought we could all leave together, but it was difficult. For my mother and my sister, it was really difficult. My elder brother told me and my younger brother that he would stay and be with our mother and sister. He said it was very dangerous for us so we should leave. My brother, my father, and I went to Iran, then to Turkey, and from Turkey to Greece. We left to find a better life.

We tried to go to Bulgaria twelve times and to Greece six times. We made it on the seventh try. We have been in Greece for about nineteen months now.

When I was a child in school, I was good at drawing, but I never thought of becoming an artist. I just liked to draw as a hobby, to express my feelings. When I came to Greece, that all changed.

There was a girl from South Africa who worked in my camp. She was very nice, and I really enjoyed being around her. She came every week with a car full of books, a moving library.

We became good friends, and I told her about my drawings. One day I asked if she could bring me a sketchbook. I could easily have bought one myself, but I wanted to draw in a notebook she gave me personally. [Laughs.]

A few weeks later, she came back with three notebooks and said, "Here are your notebooks and some pencils. I will be back next week, and I want to see what you draw." So I drew seven pieces. One for each day until I saw her again.

When I showed her my drawings, she was shocked! She asked, "Who drew these? These are amazing." She took a picture with her phone. The fact that she appreciated my work really meant a lot, and I started to draw more and more.

She left a month later. It broke my heart, but I knew I would continue to make art. Six months later, I had my first exhibit in Monastiraki in central Athens.

It was a really amazing exhibition; I showed sixteen works, and the people loved them, especially teenagers. They could relate to my work because we are all young. I made drawings with many details about life and people that they were familiar with. Older people like my social worker, my lawyer, and people from the camp also liked the work. Their support encouraged me to do more and more. They all made me an artist.

When I begin a new piece, I have to be listening to music. Without songs, I cannot draw. There were many times when I was sad, but music was always there for me. When I listen to it, it makes me happy. It helps me overcome my problems, my sadness, and other feelings. Art and music have done all of that for me.

Many refugees leave behind beautiful lives. I had a beautiful life in my country, but the war forced us to leave everything. I like to use my art to make other refugees feel better. I made many drawings and paintings showing refugees. Even if they were sad and full of conflicting emotions, my art made them feel better. Oftentimes we cannot express ourselves with words, but we can express ourselves by drawing or making a physical thing.

I also like writing. I'm not sure I could write a book, but I like creating stories and poems. Sometimes I cannot express myself well with words, so I write them down and draw from their meaning. I like to use both so people can understand my work better.

It's wrong to say that refugees are just one big group of similar people. Nobody is the same. All people are different, and that is certainly true for refugees as well. But often, if someone does ninety-nine good things and one bad thing, people say he is all bad. As is true of any group, there are good people, and there are bad people. Unfortunately, people often dwell on the bad and take the good for granted. We must be fair in our judgments. We can all be good and bad. Unfortunately, the world usually highlights the wrong people.

Young refugees should try not to be scared, and it's very important that they study. That's especially true if they have talent like many of my friends, whether it is soccer, cricket, guitar, or art. Find hobbies you like and keeping doing them. Day by day you will improve, and maybe someday you will do something great.

Everyone in my school knows me as an artist. Many students and teachers don't even know my name, but they know I'm an artist. People in the street often come up and greet me. They tell me, "You're an artist—I saw your work on Facebook." It feels really good, even though what I'm doing isn't really a big deal. Art is my hobby, and I love to do it. I'm happy to be doing something that I love and that people enjoy.

If we talk to people, we make connections, and they will know us better. When I came to Greece, I knew only my brother and a few friends from other camps. I was not connected with many people. But as an artist, now I have many friends from all around Europe and America—many friends. Every day people send me friend requests on Facebook and want to know more about me. The more connected we are, the more I hope we can improve the lives of refugees around the world.

Artwork by Jameel Khan

LOST IN JOY

LOST IN JOY (close-up)

Untitled

Stranger in the Strange Land

Criticism

Silence

Rain of Ignorance

Hate

Desperation

Untitled

"Refugees"
Talking About Afghanistan and Syria

"Refugees"
Talking About Afghanistan and Syria

* I always heard the word "Refugee". But I never imagined, I would be one. One day you are busy sending your kids off to school. Planning your older son/daughter's university applications. Teaching your own class of primary pupils and arranging dinner in your comfortable two-story home. OR go outside with your friends.

* And there, one day you just open your eyes and you are in a "Refugee Camp" with little more than the clothes you are wearing, There's nothing left of Previous life except for sharp memories.

* Your house, your cat, your parents/siblings, your friends, your children, wife/husband, education and so many [have] been taken by "Brutal Civil War".

* Our country was beautiful, our childhood was beautiful, we spend a beautiful life we never think that one day we will leave everything. We will have our house, we will have our country, our schools, our friends, our siblings, our everything. It happened we left everything behind. Some of us lost our parents, some of us lost our brothers and sisters some of us living alone. It's like still a "Nightmares" for Syrian and Afghans. Seeing your life destroyed with your eyes. It's still like "Nightmares" still it keeps us awake at night.

* We lost Everything in our life. But we still have hope. Living with Broken hearts, and Burning Souls.

Jameel Khan self-portrait

شمس

("Sun")

A tribute to Alan Kurdi

We still remember your eyes.
How they made the sea tremble.
How they reminded us that
our mothers held us in the same way.
Our fathers' shadows were just as tall.
Our ancestors shared the same breath.

Remember how the sun hugged our countries,
a golden diary for every soul, young and old?
Every page a testament to your resilience.

We carry your spirit on our growing shoulders.
We've learned to keep our memories inside so we can
emigrate with our history.
After all, our most prized possessions are the ones that can
only be taken away by God.

The sun now embraces us in a new land.
We try to return the embrace, but we hear
Aleppo's song in the distance.
We hear
Baghdad's poetry shake the ocean floor.

The cities are impatient for our return.
They speak of lost times, desperate journeys, and new worlds.
They tell us they have not forgotten.
They tell us the sun is in our hands and it's our job to return it.

We hold it with shaky palms and keep it between our shoulders.

When the time comes, the world will be as welcoming as our
mothers' hands,
as tall as the shadows of our fathers,
and as eloquent as our ancestors' tongues.

The sun will rise tomorrow and so will your spirit.

In that moment, we will hug you both.

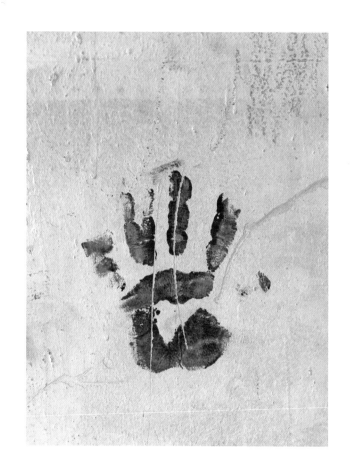

A child's handprint stamped on a wall in an abandoned building at a refugee camp north of Athens, where many of the book's works were created. This wall is part of a building on the site of a former air force base, and once housed hundreds of camp residents. After more formal living structures were established, the building fell into disrepair, and its walls became blank canvases for the camp's residents to shape and curate. The book cover photo features another wall in this building.

NOTES

Khadija Mohamed (*"Naag iska dhig"*), Eid Ahmed (*"Hooyo, Ayeeyo, Adeer"*), Abshir Habseme (*"Canjeero"*), Alfahad Tabrizi ("The Anatomy of Tyranny"), Istarlin Dafe ("The Cup of Memory"), Ibraheem Abdi ("Arrowhead"), Fidaa Aljabbarin ("Darkness and Light"), Nidaa Aljabbarin ("The Day I Left"), Nurallah Alawsaj ("We Are Returning"), and Abdirizak Noor (*"Guriga"*) were all part of the inaugural class of the Narratio Fellowship, an intensive four-week storytelling program for resettled refugee youth. Launched in collaboration with The Metropolitan Museum of Art's Ancient Near East Department, Syracuse University and the North Side Learning Center (NSLC) in Syracuse, New York, the program utilizes a multidisciplinary approach to self-expression that includes workshops, guest speakers, and site visits, culminating in a week-long trip to New York City where Fellows participate in sessions at the United Nations, Squarespace, and *The New York Times*.

Through this program, Fellows are given the opportunity to reclaim the complexity of their own narratives by embracing the plurality of their identities as new Americans, critically engaging with their personal experiences and finding new avenues for self-expression.

Each Fellow selected an object from the Metropolitan Museum's Ancient Near East Galleries and rewrote its label as a poem, taking into account personal memories, histories, and identities.

On July 31, 2019, the Fellows debuted their poems with a performance in the Royal Assyrian Court at the Metropolitan Museum of Art in New York City.

View the objects that inspired the poems and learn more about the Narratio Fellowship at www.narratio.org/fellowship.

The Narratio Fellows in Brooklyn, New York, en route to their poetry performances at The Met.

Left to right: Fellowship co-director Brice Nordquist; facilitator Adiba Alam; fellows Nurallah Alawsaj, Istarlin Dafe, Khadija Mohamed, Jamal Bilata, Eid Ahmed, Abshir Habseme, Ibraheem Abdi, Muhammad Musaab, Abdirizak Noor; and the North Side Learning Center's Hussein Yerow and Mark Cass. Not pictured: Nidaa and Fidaa Aljabbarin.

Photo by Edward Grattan.

ACKNOWLEDGMENTS

I am immensely lucky to have the support of so many incredible humans. My gratitude and appreciation for these individuals is unlimited, and every day I wake up pinching myself, realizing how privileged I am to know and interact with each and every one of these generous souls.

First, thank you to Mama, Baba, and Maryam. Your existence, resilience, and love are my life's greatest gifts. Thank you to all of my extended family in Iraq and beyond; especially my dear aunts Sanaa, Muna, and Israa. Thank you for introducing a young kid to the power of art and creative expression. Thank you to my dear uncle Yassir and aunt Manal, and my cousins Bader and Mohammad.

I will forever be grateful to my beloved grandparents Rabea, Hamid, Safiya, and Badr. May you rest in eternal peace. This is all for you.

Thank you to my best friend, Mohammad Shobaki, for showing me that brilliance and kindness go hand in hand in the quest for social justice. Thank you to Russell and Beverly Stubbles for encouraging me to tell my story way before I knew I had one to tell.

Thank you to my wonderful friends and mentors: Lloyd Winston, Ari Shapiro, Marissa Storozum, Hajer Naili, and Tom Barritt. Your presence in my life continues to inspire and motivate me to become the best version of myself.

I'm eternally grateful to the one and only Ben Stiller for writing such a beautiful foreword. Your originality, kindness, and humor have inspired the world a million times over, and I'm so honored to know and learn from you.

A mountain of thanks to my brother and friend Edward Grattan, Narratio's Managing Director, and one of the best photographers I have ever had the pleasure of meeting and working with. Eddy, your compassion, selflessness, and empathy know no bounds, and I'm so fortunate to be on this journey with you. I will always be grateful for our chance meeting during one of the very first Narratio Workshops in Greece.

Immense thanks to my dear friend Melissa Fleming and the entire UN Refugee Agency (UNHCR) team for their on-the-ground support and guidance. Thank you to the phenomenal folks at the UNHCR Offices in New York, Nairobi, Athens, Port of Spain, and London: Jennifer Abraham, Kathryn Mahoney, Joung-ah Ghedini-Williams, Nancy Aburi, Evanthia Savvopoulou, Leo Dobbs, Aikaterini Stavroula, Leila Jane Nassif, Amanda Choo Quan, Andrew Welch, Mattieu Ramsawak, Sarah Epstein, and Coco Campbell.

My time in Greece (and this book) would not have been possible without the support of Mohammed Jopran Alsaied and Niamh Keady Tabbal. Thank you for being so considerate and understanding, and for guiding me through the country with respect and humility. Thank you to Lighthouse Relief and their extraordinary Youth Engagement Space (YES) for allowing me to bring Narratio into your camp. Special thanks to Meg O'Neill, Valentina Giudizio, Natasha

Crickmore, and Keelin Macdonald. Thank you to Aanjalie Roane for introducing me to Lighthouse and its critical, selfless work.

Thank you to Jess Teutonico, Nancy Hunt, Annie Greene, Ali Kaplan, and the entire We Are Family Foundation. Your constant support and advice means the world to me, and I will always be proud to be part of the family.

Thank you to my Wesleyan University advisers, mentors, professors, and friends for putting up with me and my wildly ambitious projects with the utmost patience, kindness, and care. Special thanks to Makaela Kingsley, Alice Hadler, and Rani Arbo. Thank you for showing me the way, and encouraging me to dive into my deepest passions with your unforgettable energy and advice. Thank you to professors Joseph Weiss, Margot Weiss, Lisa Dombrowski, Ronald Jenkins, Elizabeth Traube, Anu Sharma, Peter Rutland, Tracy Strain, and Lauren Rosewarne for your kind and thoughtful lessons and conversations. Thank you to Bob Patricelli and the Patricelli Center for Social Entrepreneurship for believing in Narratio's mission and supporting our programs.

Thank you to my dear friends and classmates Raul Covarrubias, AJ Wilson, Thafir Elzofri, Hira Jafri, Kofi Ofori-Darko, Giorgia Sage, Stefano Castro, Annie Ning, Maximillien Chong Lee Shin, Yussra Hamid, and Russell Reed for being a constant source of love, kindness, and bad jokes. Thank you to the remarkable Jesse Galganov; I was so lucky to know you during your time at Wesleyan, and will always cherish our memories; I sincerely hope to see you again one day.

Thank you to Shay Odimayo and Khoa Truong for supporting Narratio in our earliest form. Thank you to all who made the Narratio Fellowship a reality. A very special thanks to Brice Nordquist, the best collaborator anyone could ask for: I am so lucky to be able to work and learn alongside you, and sincerely appreciate your warmth, thoughtfulness, and humor. Thank you to Syracuse University and Professor Eileen Schell for introducing me to your marvelous city. Thank you to our first Fellowship partner, the North Side Learning Center (NSLC), and its Executive Director, Mark Cass, for supporting the program from the very beginning. The program would not have been possible without our superb facilitators: Gemma Cooper-Novack, Elang Basadi, and Adiba Alam. Your hard work is much appreciated.

Thank you to the Metropolitan Museum of Art's Ancient Near East Department for opening your doors and objects to the Fellowship. A very special thanks to Sarah Graff, and her unparalleled thoughtfulness and enthusiasm. Thank you, Kim Benzel and Lea St-Arnaud-Boffa, for trusting our vision and working tirelessly to make it a reality.

Thank you to my spectacular editor, Melissa Rhodes Zahorsky, for her patience, attention to detail, and appreciation of nuance; it has been an absolute pleasure to work on this project with you. Thank you to the amazing Kirsty Melville and the entire Andrews McMeel team for believing in this project and for giving refugee youth a chance to showcase their work on the global stage. This is only the beginning.

Additional thanks to these wonderful friends, collaborators, and supporters: Merzad Shixe and his beautiful family, Ali Hamza, Fars

Zaxoli (and his extraordinary Falafel restaurant), Jenifer Fenton, Mohamad Hafez, Celine Cunha, Matthew Capasso, Sotiris Sideris and the Young Journalists, Diktio, Migratory Birds newspaper, the recording studios of the National Library of Greece, Maher Nasser, The Office of Secretary General's Envoy on Youth, Jayathma Wickramanayke, Sheryl Winarick, Tolu Olubunmi, 2016-17 WeSlam poetry team at Wesleyan University, Leonard Doyle and the International Organization for Migration (IOM), Richard Davies, Abdirahman Olow, Rahma Gamil, Alex Cromwell, Leslie Dwyer, Degung Santikarma, Andrew Barrett, John Augillard, Chrystal Carrizal Limon, Jennifer Johnson, Kathy Eads, Bob Daugherty, Andy Kirkpatrick, and George Mason University.

Last but certainly not least, thank you to all of the individuals featured in this book. Thank you for trusting me with your expression, and thank you for choosing to believe in the power of storytelling.

Andrews McMeel Publishing
a division of Andrews McMeel Universal
1130 Walnut Street, Kansas City, Missouri 64106

www.andrewsmcmeel.com

www.earthsleepswetravel.com

www.ahmedmbadr.com

20 21 22 23 24 TEN 10 9 8 7 6 5 4 3 2 1

ISBN: 978-1-4494-9642-5

Library of Congress Control Number: 2020938398

Editor: Melissa Rhodes Zahorsky
Art Director: Tiffany Meairs
Production Editor: Jasmine Lim
Production Manager: Carol Coe

ATTENTION: SCHOOLS AND BUSINESSES
Andrews McMeel books are available at quantity discounts with
bulk purchase for educational, business, or sales promotional use.
For information, please e-mail the Andrews McMeel Publishing
Special Sales Department: specialsales@amuniversal.com.

The views and opinions expressed do not necessarily reflect
the official policy or position of any of the organizations,
institutions, and agencies mentioned in the book.

A percentage of author royalties will be donated to
initiatives and organizations supporting programming and
publishing for displaced young people across the world.